A Field Guide to the Spirits

Conversation Pieces

A Small Paperback Series from Aqueduct Press
Subscriptions available: www.aqueductpress.com

About the Aqueduct Press
Conversation Pieces Series

The feminist engaged with sf is passionately interested in challenging the way things are, passionately determined to understand how everything works. It is my constant sense of our feminist-sf present as a grand conversation that enables me to trace its existence into the past and from there see its trajectory extending into our future. A genealogy for feminist sf would not constitute a chart depicting direct lineages but would offer us an ever-shifting, fluid mosaic, the individual tiles of which we will probably only ever partially access. What could be more in the spirit of feminist sf than to conceptualize a genealogy that explicitly manifests our own communities across not only space but also time?

Aqueduct's small paperback series, Conversation Pieces, aims to both document and facilitate the "grand conversation." The Conversation Pieces series presents a wide variety of texts, including short fiction (which may not always be sf and may not necessarily even be feminist), essays, speeches, manifestoes, poetry, interviews, correspondence, and group discussions. Many of the texts are reprinted material, but some are new. The grand conversation reaches at least as far back as Mary Shelley and extends, in our speculations and visions, into the continually-created future. In Jonathan Goldberg's words, "To look forward to the history that will be, one must look at and retell the history that has been told." And that is what Conversation Pieces is all about.

L. Timmel Duchamp

Jonathan Goldberg, "The History That Will Be" in Louise Fradenburg and Carla Freccero, eds., *Premodern Sexualities* (New York and London: Routledge, 1996)

Published by Aqueduct Press
PO Box 95787
Seattle, WA 98145-2787
www.aqueductpress.com

10 9 8 7 6 5 4 3 2 1
ISBN: 978-1-61976 097-4
All illustrations copyright © 2015 by Jean LeBlanc

Original Block Print of Mary Shelley by Justin Kempton:
www.writersmugs.com

Printed in the USA by Applied Digital Imaging

Conversation Pieces
Volume 47

A Field Guide to the Spirits

Poems by
Jean LeBlanc

Acknowledgments
Previous publications

"In Memory," *Albatross*, issue #23, 2012.

"When the Self Goes, It Goes," *Bellevue Literary Review*, Volume 11, No. 2, Fall 2011.

"Our Maladies," *Bellevue Literary Review*, Volume 13, No. 1, Spring 2013.

"The Plague Stone," *Community College Moment*, Volume 13, Spring 2013.

"Dashiell Hammett, Age 57, Reads *Jane Eyre* in the Ashland Federal Correctional Institution, Ashland, Kentucky, 1951," and "William James and Sigmund Freud Walk to the Train Station, Worcester, Massachusetts, 1909, " *Community College Moment*, Volume 15, Spring 2015.

"How the Smith Boys Died, and When," *Journal of New Jersey Poets*, Spring, 1999.

"What if Your Dentist Were Zane Grey" and "William Blake Teaches His Wife to Read," *The Journal of Pedagogy, Pluralism and Practice*, Fall, 2014.

"Katherine Wheelwright Nanny Naylor's Privy," *Off the Coast*, Winter, 2012.

"Ptolemy Prepares to Read a Friend's Astrology," *Taj Mahal Review*, Volume 12, No. 1, June 2013.

"Cleopatra's Snake Girl," *Third Wednesday*, Winter 2011.

"Split Rock," *You Are Here*, 2012.

To those who haunt us,
and to those whom we will haunt hereafter.

Contents

Know Your Spirits

He never was the type to overturn a table.
There was that time—but no, he is too much
the gentleman to send that message, says you'll
remember. There's another presence here,
who could toss a chair or two, not in anger,
simply to make us aware. Will any claim him,
this unsettled visitor? No spirit ever says,
I loved you not. For all the earthly matches
forged in hell, every departed soul's a dear.
Not one admits, *I am less dead now.*
This message never comes: *Stop haunting me
from your dark and winter world.*

Great Interest in Our Underthings

The town's First Citizens had us stand on tables so they
didn't have to strain. A close and scientific inspection,
they called it. A windowless room. Great interest in
our underthings. Fold upon fold of fabric in which
to secrete stones, or iron, or wooden blocks. Every
inch. And then went over us again. Finding naught.
Greater interest still in foot and ankle, knee and. And.
Hands that fumbled with. Stopped just shy of. Their
faces so close to. Unconvinced, return to pocket, seam,
and hem. Certain something had been overlooked. A
squirm, a start, a sudden breath—little hints that they
were close. Only to disappoint. *In the matter of veracity
we have our doubts, but we could not disprove.* They searched
and searched for secrets. We discovered theirs.

What We Really Mean
When We Say "Love"

Hate. But that's too easy. It's more than that.
You got the way the rooted earth folds itself
over the edge of the cliff, the cliff a good three feet
farther back beneath, but that flap of sod holds on.
You got the neighbor boy running down a hill
and suddenly you think of the day your father died,
the way you felt in that boy's posture—his of joy,
yours of pain, the same thing. The coat on its hook.
Buttonwood bark. The sheen on the buckets
in the spring house. Go on and nod at the word
"hate." But the taste of water from those buckets,
it's enough to make an old man determine to see
one more summer. Love means dying when
the ground is froze. Love means digging that hole.

Photographing Snowflakes

The right kind of storm, not so cold
it's all pellets, but up near freezing,
allowing the crystals time to grow,

spikes and spires and plates branching out
in six directions, the desire for symmetry
apparent, though rarely realized.

The ones that land upright—look for those,
assuming you have eyes for something
almost clear and tiny and easily broken.

Up near freezing, but not. They might
last the few moments it takes to focus.
And as for breathing, don't. Funny,

the word "ephemeral." Just as you
think it, it proves its point. Hold
your breath as if the flake could hear you

getting close. Hold your breath as if you had
discovered the secret to eternal life.
Hold your breath as, even then, it slips away.

Katherine Wheelwright
Nanny Naylor's Privy

—excavated by archaeologists during the 1990s
Central Artery Project in Boston, Massachusetts

The biggest mystery is the bowling ball,
a decidedly un-Puritan pastime. A lesson,
perhaps, of what such godless pursuits
do to one's immortal soul? Easier
to understand the daily objects too easily
lost from shallow pockets, or dropped
from a string around one's waist: the keys,
the belt buckle, the little pincushion.
Still, the bowling ball has good company,
what with all the mysteries down there,
like a candle holder and pewter spoons.
And it is a redolent topic overall,
and makes one glad today of our privilege
to flush, so as not, three hundred and fifty
years from now, to be known by what
we have left, *ahem*, behind. Better to imagine
from the hundred thousand cherry pits,
a Boston summer, the harbor visible
from the house back then, the sea breeze
soothing the sleepers, full of mutton
and fruit pie, even the child who had cried
herself to sleep, knowing she was in for it,

having dropped her little goat-skin shoe
down there, so sure that God would
catch it, and give it back, now not knowing
what to fear more: this evidence of God's
silent wrath, or her mother's
not-so-silent wrath to come.

Marie, *sans* Pierre

After the commotion, after the men's shouts
and the women's screams, after the untangling
of hooves and loosening of clothing,
after the blood on the cobblestones,
after the last utterance of *mon dieu*,

to stand again in the laboratory, amongst
the familiar *accoutrement*, to see, perhaps,
the pencil he had left on the bench, intending—
Non, ne pense pas, seulement travailler,
travailler pour deux.

Jean LeBlanc

Last Words

Yes, yes, Billy—you go down that side of Long Pond, and
I'll go this side and we'll get some ducks—
—John James Audubon's last words,
spoken to his brother-in-law William Blakewell

When the water was not too high, not too low,
we could stretch out on the soft wide planks
and watch the river light dance on the trees,
a tunnel of trees, a dense, greenshadowed life,
an amber sunbeam here and there, and birds, and birds,
and insectsong, and the slow pull of the river,
The Ohio by flat-bottomed boat, just current and hope,
and someone would strum a banjo, and we would doze,
too young to feel the ache in the bones, even chill nights,
even after jumping overboard to push our floating world
over snags and sandbars, downstream, down,
a herd of deer swimming across, the owls on patrol,
the freedom, the freedom from freedom, each evening
the same last words: *Today, then, we have seen it all.*

Hope, Hunger, Birds

*They are very much their own enemies, in this way, for
no birds are greater fruit-eaters than themselves; they are
even voracious feeders when they find a berry to their taste,
actually destroying themselves, at times, by the numbers
they swallow.*
—*Susan Fenimore Cooper,* Rural Hours

Like the cedar waxwings, so delicate-looking,
so dapper, but oh what profligates, what gluttons
both for bloom and for fruit, not knowing, it seems,
when to stop, stuffing themselves on juniper
until drunk, then flying into windows, breaking
their necks. Like a songbird, my old heart,
still believing it will see another spring, craving
every tender blossom, wanting more.
When are we too old for love, I wonder?
When do we look ridiculous, making eyes
and sighing, feasting on hope, unaware
that an excess of that fine feeling can,
like fermented fruit after the first frost,
kill us sure as grief? Does one die smiling,
drunk on hope, one's little neck snapped in two
against the pane? One cannot be warned off.
It is impossible to say, "Not one more dream."
Tell the bobolinks nesting in the meadow
that the railroad just mapped out the right-of-way,
and you will see them, on the morrow, gathering

long bits of grass to make some small repairs.
Then see them in every last frantic, swooping whirl
above the heads of the crew come with picks and shovels,
until the meadow is no more. And what of hope?
I must believe we carry it with us, on that final flight,
a length of straw wrapped in our beaks, hearts bursting
as we sing, *I shall make another, make another, make another life.*

Automatic Writing

The first time a spirit took my hand
and guided it across the page, even I
was doubtful, thinking the effort
must be mine and mine alone.
But how to explain the presence,
the touch, the sense that my own arm
was, for the moment, not fully
in my control—I was the scribe,
while the volition came from without.
I am pleased when a spirit
has me pen, *Darling, I love you still.*
Sometimes, there are the mysteries
to solve: *Look again through*
all the drawers; the key you seek is there,
unless it was discarded with my things.
Often, a note of comfort is passed:
We wait for you; take your time.
Two spirits seize me, one right, one left—
We are all young here
and the other, *.llew era eW*

The Way To and From Forever

You are not certain, not certain at all, but
sometimes it feels as if you have found it.
For a moment, you and the heron share
a little stretch of shoreline. You witness
the first flight of a damselfly, wings newly
wings. A few fish the length of your forearm
pause in the shallows. There are more hints,
if you wait for them, of this path you never
really leave. Maybe, too, you have a friend
who listens when you say such things, who
holds one of your hands while you reach
the other out beyond the singularity, to pull you
back or fall in with you. The heron flies off,
low over the water, as if challenging you
to follow. You cannot. But you watch
as gray-blue bird becomes gray-blue horizon,
and you think, *That I can do.*

Ptolemy Prepares to Read
a Friend's Astrology

Once they know you know the stars,
they pester and pester. I try to explain
there are many things that shape
the future: where they were born,
what metal object they last touched,
the interwoven fates of everyone
in their household: spouse, children,
aging parents, servants, dogs.
Influence upon influence. Still,
they ask me to tell them their stars.
And so, I tell them. *Watch out*
for the chambermaid with watery eyes.
Sell her to your enemy. The goats
you receive as payment—turn them
loose in the street before they overrun
your yard with fleas. Practical advice,
words so general they go home nodding,
glad that they have seen ahead, pleased
the night sky is a great book, the gods
swayable by an old man with a few charts
and a scholar's crooked back.

Free Will

You can get married on the balcony
where the realish Romeo wooed
the realish Juliet. Best not to read
too much further into that story. If
you're marrying in public, chances are
your families are not consumed
by a blood vendetta. Chances are
the priest has not slipped anyone
a potion to mimic death. Still,
you'd have to be more than a little
brave, to step out onto that balcony
and not imagine you hear, at the end
of the lovely vows, *Thus with a kiss I die.*

How Else Could Kate Fox Know Your Secrets

unless the spirits themselves were spelling them out for her—for all—to hear? Even the most hardened skeptic leaves a little shaken, having heard described the way a lover touched palm to cheek, how that touch led to the most delicate of kisses—*delicate*, and then the spirit spells out *intimate*, and chairs are overturned, whether from the spirits aching with earthly desire or the no-longer-quite-so-skeptical wanting to put an end—

Kate Fox goes all translucent, as if joining the spirit world, becoming one of them, and another insists on being heard, and another, and still do you not quite believe? Your lover knew all along that you thought at first, *What funny little fingers, funny little hands*, but not long thereafter you worshipped those hands, as they found their way, found their way, found their delicate, intimate, secret way.

To Live Like the Polypody Fern

No better companions, moss and rock,
sun and rain. Find a place just *so*,
the light not *too*, the shade not *very*.
If you must be exposed, be secret.
If you are tucked away, declare
yourself the arbiter of green.
Gneiss or limestone, either or.
To have been admired by Thoreau.
To have known what it feels like
to unfurl. The deep quiet of woods,
the pileated's persistent din.
To live like that, between earth and sky.
Sometimes the good is in the getting by.

March Conversation

This time of year all the world's a slough.
     Gone milky with mud.
A feckless fen.
     Snowmelt can't sink in, liquids every field.
Wanton water seeps into every seem.
     Unseemly, to be always so wet, yet cold.
The ice retreats.
     Gardeners retreat, as well.
Too soon, too soon.
     Cold frames fill.
Tendrils blanch and curl against false sky.
     A good hard frost sows seeds of remorse.
I saw water tumbling—*tumbling*—down a hill!
     First storm fills the Narrows.
Ducks in the street.
     To our knees in mud, to our knees in trout.
Your father say that?
     Grandfather.
Bless his sodden heart.

Caroline Herschel, Twelve Years Old

I wake up before the sun, to light the fire
and thaw the water. I fill a basin, wash
my face and little arms. I have named
the constellations of my smallpox scars.
There's Lorelei, her mermaid tail, and Holda,
goddess of spinning. I imagine the sweet words
they would say. *Keep swimming, little sprite,
keep swimming to where the current is strong,
and can carry you. Keep sewing, sweet spirit,
keep sewing, and one day the thread you pull
will be your own life, your own life.* And then
I roll my sleeves down, over Lorelei and Holda,
and begin the day's baking, warm at last.

Caroline Herschel on the Journey from Hanover to Bath

I am the same size as a sack of letters,
so on the mail coach mile after mile
I can just curl up and sleep. Nights,
though, William lifts me to the top,
where he holds on to me so I don't
bounce off. He teaches me Orion
and the secrets of the Moon. The driver
clicking to the horses, the clatter
of hooves—William points out
stars that are not single stars, but pairs,
or clouds of stars, and describes
what I will see with his telescope.
Imagine: last week I knew nothing.
Now I can speak of reflectors
and refractors, of Betelgeuse and
Rigel. I love traveling. I can wear
a veil to hide my face, and I feel
at last I am something in this universe,
a small something, but the driver
tips his hat to me, thanks my brother
for having named the stars. We
may drown crossing the Channel,
but as I die, I will think of
some other Caroline, living
on the Moon, looking up at me,

and I will tell her, *Learn all you can,*
learn the name of every single thing,
for briefly, briefly, it is ours.

Caroline Herschel at Ninety-Eight

She is four foot, three inches tall.
She has telescopes to bring the stars
to her. Sir Joseph Banks would visit,
spend the afternoon telling her
about Tahiti, the transit of Venus,
Australia. At Kew, he plucked
and handed her a fresh sprig
of eucalyptus, bowing extra low
to indicate it was not her height,
but his great honor, to offer it.
Caroline is four foot, three inches
tall, her face scarred from smallpox.
Multiplication tables have always
vexed her. *Seven eights is fifty-four—*
no, fifty-six, why am I such a dunce?
Comet after comet, and all for him,
all for him, she might mumble
on her deathbed, in German, those
at her side not understanding, thinking
only, *How wonderful to live almost*
one hundred years, to have seen
what she has seen, the name Herschel
in the heavens, beloved by all. Her fingers
move at her side, counting out sevens,
then eights. *Clouds, will there be clouds*
tonight? A dried sprig pressed
in a handkerchief, in her tiny hand.
Four foot three. Her fingers, at last, still.

William Caxton Encourages
an Apprentice

Carve the serif in wood then cast the lot in metal,
spur after little spur, the corners sharp but no gloves
in this job, you need your fingers free, the only tools
that count, them and eyes, and build letter by letter the
Histories of Troye returned to full glorious life, drawn
out of French into English, English broad and rude
and crass and strange and base and bastard for all that,
English of many tongues made one, and fit and fair,
and if you keep your senses through this close and
backward work, your poor ghost—yes, an aitch, that's
right—your poor ghost will one day spell out for the
angels all there is to say in this world, and the next.

Gout

The vine that has never bloomed since he planted it
blooms just before Sir Joseph has himself wheeled
one last time through the orangery at Kew. There are
a few dried petals on the floor, and he can see
the little cuplets where the flowers were. Hundreds
of flowers. His mind drifts back to Tahiti, everything
always in bloom, always more just about to open.
That was where he found the parent to this vine.
He can almost recall the flowers, purple, or was it
pink, or magenta, one of those hues, and oh, his
island wife, her velvet thighs, naked afternoons,
his skin almost as brown as hers, not like now,
the pain, this wheelchair, companions long dead,
Captain Cook's body divided up among the chiefs.

Joseph Banks Describes Tahiti to Samuel Taylor Coleridge

Even the sand was beautiful, every grain
a pearl. And how they loved the ocean,
could ride the breakers standing up
on worn-away canoes, just boards really.
Just for the joy of it, and we watched
just for the delight of seeing. I drank the milk
of Paradise, and lived to tell of it. I was Adam,
I had my Eve, and every night we fell,
and every morning we arose to the same lush,
generous, verdant life. Thank God I dream
in color, and can visit when I close my eyes.
On honeydew I have feasted, under a different sun,
on a different, smaller, larger sun-washed world.

You Don't Want to Be Like That

The boy who dies when the car
he's driving slams into a tree—
and when it's in the local paper
the next day, everyone is surprised,
because they thought he had died
ten years earlier sledding on
a snow-covered street and out
into traffic. People mistake
someone else's death for yours,
my mother says. You don't want
to be like that. And then when
you do die, people are too confused
to mourn, not that they mourned him
much to begin with. She isn't really
talking to me. I'm doing my geometry,
and I'll be sitting up late reading
The Mill on the Floss. I don't cause
trouble. I don't even have my
learner's permit. I walk to school,
to tennis practice, home. I may be
a little lax in keeping my room
tidy. People may very well ask,
when I die, Didn't she die years ago?

Autopsy

Because she cannot bear to go to her grave thinking
he might have gone to his enthralled of Satan, as
the entire town whispered, his behavior in his final months

proof thereof—because of this, she asks the doctor to open
his brain and breast—seat of reason, home of the soul—
and allow her to observe. What wife would not do as much

to absolve, even secretly, a devoted spouse? Because
he had loved her once, had asked for her hand knowing
her father would deride a country sawbone's suit,

the doctor agrees, though if this thing were public
he would be run out of state, or worse. She tells
only her journal: *the blade rasped into the skull—*

the blackened mass within—From Satan's hand?—
No. Cancer—an odd comfort, this; a trial from God
he bore as well as any could. And then: *His breastbone,*

radiant, giving off more light than may be explained
by mirrored candles in a windowless inner room.
A sign his soul indeed has found that better place.

Now the Field Is Cold
where Last Spring

water snakes came to sun, entwined
each around each in dappled light. We

aren't much more than strangers, and yet
we speak of emptiness. Last year the first

turning of earth met with all those turtles
laying eggs. This, then, is the year after

that particular massacre. Little more than
strangers, speaking of migration and weather.

I was a ghost once, I would tell you, if you
were to ask. You would know what I meant.

Something pulled me back, recommending
flesh. Flesh and bone and gristle and ache.

Medium

she wanted to tell you this before / wants to tell you
now / she is grateful for every word / all those months
of her dying / every word you spoke / expressions of
love / stories of the past / descriptions of the weather
/ nothing so mundane that she did not love to hear
it from your lips / it made her sad to be leaving / to
be unable to respond / though she was also sorry to
be taking so long / lingering / her heart the healthiest
thing left / yes even with that little murmur / the
pulse so reluctant to forsake that lovely wrist / she
wanted to move her hand just so / in that way she
had / to show you she could hear / those poems you
recited / please / she asks / give a line or two now /
yes / that one / that one especially / she remembers
that very afternoon / clouds across the window /
sun then no sun then sun again / or perhaps it was a
storm / a singular light / even with the blinds closed
she could sense it / and you searching desperately
for words / you bowed your head / looked up at the
ceiling / perhaps closed your eyes / those lines / that
poem / others / every word you spoke / including the
unspoken ones /

Moonflower

The involutions of a mind
still so beautiful around the edges.

Calling loved ones "Love."
Adjusting the window shades.

A department store aisle
walked a hundred times before
is new.

Today's blue sky
the first sky ever.

My father, her father, her stepfather
all home from the hospital at once—
no, not at once exactly,
not home exactly,
but all here.

Adjusting the window shades again
though there is no one to see in.

The moonflower in the evening.
A movement one wishes could be called
an opening.

An opening, an opening. Then,
night.

Vento et Rapida

My class, researching Catullus, can find
only vague references to his having died
of "exhaustion," and although
these are college students, adults,
we change the subject, too timid to speculate
on the ways of tiring a young man to death.
"Wind and running water, his life
was written on wind and running water,"
one woman says, quoting a phrase
from his poems. O, the final taste
of wine, the final kiss, the final touch
of cool, smooth marble on a fevered brow.

How the Smith Boys Died, and When

To be honest, gravestones tell us nothing.
Here in the mountains of Vermont we can read
the south-facing side of the Smith family marker
and learn that Perley, son of D.W. and Ella,
was killed on July 4, 1894, by the explosion of a cannon.
We cannot know if he awoke that morning
with a sense of dread, if he shrugged it off as nerves
over his part in the festivities.
Will I fire the cannon off too soon?
Will I flinch at the sound?
Or was it on a dare that this sixteen-year-old boy
stood close enough to feel the boom take hold of his heart
Should I cover my ears, or is that sissy?
On the same face of the same stone we can read that
Perley's brother Winfield, at age 19,
had died in January that same year
beneath an overturning load of lumber.
A winter loss, a summer loss—was each felt the same
by Ella, who lived another thirty-six winters,
or D.W., who lived another five July Fourths beyond her?
Their dates are carved in the west side of the stone,
a stone cooled by the morning shade of maples,
the afternoon shade of cedars.
That is all we can ever know.

William Blake Teaches
His Wife to Read

> *One thought fills immensity.*
> —*William Blake*

A is for Adam; this garden is ours:
B for the bee with silvery wings,
C for the catmint, a fragrant delight,
D is daffodil in spring, daisy in summer.

E, that's you, dear Eve, cleansed of sin,
F, forget-me-not, the mouse's ear,
and G the gladiolus, sword unsheathed,
H for hollyhock, hydrangea, heaven, hell.

I is ivy twining up the wall,
J's June, July, the joyful months,
K, the graceful kestrel soaring high,
L, with love and lilies fill your arms.

M, the moths at night, those secret souls,
N, the night itself, when most blooms fade,
O, open once again, and see the sun,
P—perfection; no commandments here.

Q, the quince our English clime dislikes,
but R, the rose a rainy day embraces.
S is for sweet William (ah! you smile!),
T, for tulips men have lost their minds.

U is understanding, in heart and mind,
V—let us have violets, violets everywhere!
W, most wonderful and wild,
X, the criss-cross of the pruning shears.

Y is yarrow, nodding in field,
Z, the zephyr, refreshing on the brow.
Let us peruse again our teeming world,
Where I can see because you have eyes.

In the Neighborhood of the Mind

Hazel Street in the snow, and two little girls
so proud of their new plaid coats, their stepfather

able to build houses—entire houses—not
like their real father, who sits and drinks

and has a new family, who do not have
new coats for the winter. Our own house,

at the end of Bernice Avenue, with sheds
and chickens and gardens and an apple tree

and a swing. And then Patty died of the sugar
diabetes, and Paula and I would walk

to King's Corner, which is where I'm going
now, it's right up the street, not a mile,

and the new shopping mall, he built that too.
And I'm going to call him, and he'll come get me

and take me home, to Hazel Street, that's where
I live, not here like they keep saying. Not here.

The Forgotten Language
of the Dead City

The inhabitants ruined their soil, plowing
and plowing until the wind had nothing more
to move. Rain formed little rivulets over bare
stone, carved little tracks. There were no more
springs. Perhaps the city's name at one time
could have translated as "Happiness." We will
never know. Perhaps they changed the name
to something like "Despair," in the later days
when no one wanted to be mayor. Perhaps
their word for "mayor" became "scapegoat."
Or "scarer-away of food." Something you
would not want your neighbors to call you.
The first word to be forgotten was the word
for the opposite of "thirst."

Cleopatra's Snake Girl

I keep my hair short, couldn't stand a braid
hung down my back or coiled about my head.
I see snakes in every shadow, every curve:
a mother's arms wrapped tight around her child,
lovers embracing, supple dancers' legs.
Once I could make men stare—all it took was
a live watersnake bracelet, forked tongue
lapping the sun's warmth from my bare shoulder.
My talent prompted a royal command.
At dusk, as the day's heat lifts from the sand,
with mice as bait, I coax asps into jars
and take them to her, these dangerous toys.
At dawn I watch the gloomy Nile turn blue.
No man wants me because of what I do.

The Plague Stone

Half-way between two villages,
a smooth stone, its top a bit concave,
to fill with vinegar, in which to dip
one's fingers, spritz the air. Also,
the stone marks the place to leave
some fresh-baked loaves, meat pies,
a few sweets for the children, if
there are any children left. A way
for one village to help its neighbor
in times of quarantine. Here, then,
a basket filled with scones, a keg
of home-brewed beer. Walk back
toward the woods, and turn, and see
a trembling figure take a scone,
then take what they can carry, back
misfortune's way. Next week,
the giving may be backward, them
to us. Both sides know these things:
Always burn the baskets, never use
the same one twice. Never send
the strongest body to the stone, for they
may just keep walking, and are like to disappear.
And in good times, when the plague stone
sees no food, it is, instead, a place for travelers
to pass in silence, glad for the normal pangs
of hunger that hie them on their way.

Split Rock

Split rocks are not uncommon in our northern woods,
boulders moved by glacier and then halved by frost.
Trails wind through them, thrilling children,
who are drawn to such things, cozy places
where the imagination is set free. *I am inside
a stone,* one child might make believe, looking up
to see the narrow strip of sky or pine, the remains
of the non-stone world. Just so, in the Dutch colony
of New Amsterdam, where nine-year-old
Susan Hutchinson has stolen a few minutes
from the busy household, the press of siblings,
the endless prayers of a rebel mother whose beliefs
have brought them here, among strangers, stolen
into the woods to sit between the halves of
Split Rock, a handful of blueberries picked
along the way, a treat for any child, except today,
screams from the distance, then silence, then smoke,
and then the hands that pluck her, too, from this
known world, carry her to a new life, and she
survives, but never knows quite why. Grown
and with a family of her own, one day she opens,
as she had seen her mother do, the Bible,
just opens to any random page, though it is not
random, it is God's guidance—*there will be an answer
here*—and finds, "To whom coming as unto
a living stone, disallowed of men, but chosen of God
and precious," closes the book, listens hard, listens
to the sounds of her own children, playing in the yard.

Anne Hutchinson in the State Hospital for the Criminally Insane

Every morning, whichever sink I choose
in the long double row of sinks, I see
myself when I look up after splashing
cold water on my face. These sinks
were white once, but there is iron
in the water. I used to try to tell them—
anyone who would take me by the arm
and lead me down long hallways lined
with hooks—I used to try to make them
understand, *I am a new creature, I am
a new creature*, but the only semblance
of a response I got was *Yes, dear, whatever
you say, dear*, so even I went silent.
At shift change they tell one another,
*She was no trouble today. She is easily
redirected.* Around every corner,
I do not tell them, I see the face
of God. The water does not look rusty,
but there is iron in it still. I bring it to
my mouth, and drink, and drink.

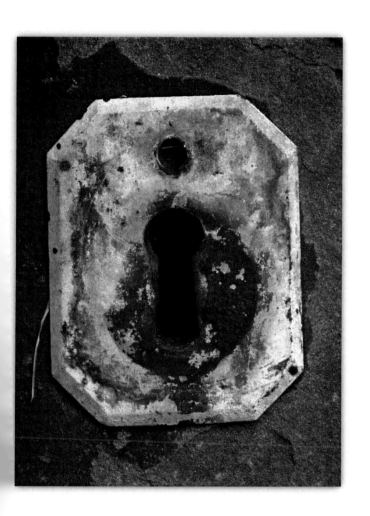

When the Self Goes, It Goes

into the folds of the purple iris which, at dawn,
becomes the hub for spider silk, filament after
filament, along one of which if you look closely

enough you can almost see the self making
its nimble way, laughing in the breeze
as the self is wont to do, the laughing self,

the nimble, laughing self, young again,
the spring flowers unstoppable now,
the self smaller than the yellow center

of a forget-me-not, and wasn't there a stream
here, it can't be dry already, so early in the year,
it is spring and we are nimble and laughing,

and we have these silken threads to guide us,
and everyone we have ever loved is here
in this garden, waving, calling the self by name.

With All that Has Been Written about the Soul

How to believe, that all along, it really was
as Lucretius said, more water than water,
more air than air, as material, though, as

a crinkled sepia photograph torn and a face
obliterated, some obscure relation gone forever
from the backyard party, their face removed but

their solid mass still holding a drink, a plate of food,
a festive slice of cake, but no mouth
with which to eat, no mouth from which the soul

can make its escape at the appointed hour,
float on up to where we believed souls go,
to mill about and warm up against the others,

a journey begun in the years of shuffling
even before death, the *here you take
these photos, I'll take those, those we'll send*

to the kids, and an envelope is misplaced,
and it is that easy, precisely that easy,
that we are lost along with it, into the nameless,

dark, frozen place of used souls, no one to write
on the back of each, "How he loved to laugh," or
"This is Mother, playing her favorite hymn."

Headwaters

I miss you most when I remember
Fallulah Brook, how it made
its delicate way through a glacial ravine
looking for all the world as if it
had sliced the granite of that hill, granite
too much even for the town fathers
who let a planned and already-mapped
road end in a cul-de-sac despite
assurances it would curve back
and meet Upper Rindge Road.
But the brook had its ravine,
its canyon through a hemlock grove.
It had its way. Thinking of the cool
and weeping stone, thinking of
the nodding ferns and mosses
that never knew the sun, thinking
of a lone bird that thought to drink
from this clear water, but, finding
the silence too deep even for
a silent woodland mind, let its wingbeats
re-announce it to the world, thinking
of this unexpected shade, I shiver,
and think of you, and I find I cannot fly
as far as I would wish from darkness,
that the sun is something I saw once
from my nest, before I fell and fell.

When Bones Speak

When bones speak, they say, *I was the femur*
of a fisherman. Or, *I was the femur of a shepherd.*
Or, *I was the skull of a well-fed villager.*

And so carefully folded, so tenderly placed,
as if sleeping—*oh loveliest of beliefs*—
sleeping with their dolls, their earthen pots,

the things they will need again, these bones.
Look at us, the skulls all say. *No crushing blows.*
We were peaceful in life, as well.

Hee Is Paile

—written by twelve-year-old Isaac Newton
in an exercise book

Away at school, boarding with the apothecary
who lets him borrow books, alone and friendless
—this is not so bad. The apothecary is kind, but
as part of his board young Isaac is required to help
replenish stock. Down to the muddy pond where
no one bathes, he bares his arm to gather leeches.
At night, he dreams of turning mud to gold, knowing
the answer is there before his eyes, so close. What he
would do with gold, he cannot quite decide. A library,
to be sure, no visitors, no older boys to torment him,
no mothers or sisters, no women at all. No one. Zero.
Well, one: himself. It isn't for the gold, it's for
the knowing how. Oh to possess that secret. He practices
his letters. *I cannot but weepe. I know not what to doe.*

Isaac Newton's Niece Catherine Barton Explains the Apple

I only meant the orchard as a whole,
where he sat month by month, those years when plague
in town forced his understanding homeward,
though he neglected all work on the farm,
let sheep browse the kitchen garden bald,
let the fish-weirs crumble, and if apples
hadn't reddened of their own accord, green
they'd be today. But there he rested, ripe
with thought, staring straight up at them, the sun
beyond, or, at night, the moon, the lights
of heaven, until they merged—apples, stars—
and that is what I meant when I should have said
the orchard's where the mystery, for him,
bore fruit, and all but dropped down on his head.

In Memory

In memory of Rachel Blank daughter of James and Matilda
Blank who departed this Life August 25th 1803
aged 5 years and 19 days
    —gravestone at Trinity Church, New York City

When you arrived at the path through the meadow
but could not go three steps in, the way blocked
by web after web, glimmering in the morning sun,

a fat spider in the center of each, what did the old woman—
herself a child come over from England, and never
letting go of the terror of that crossing, the vast nothing

called sea, the voice of death in the creak of every timber—
what did she say, something about *an omen, she'll go*
not much further through life, saying this just as you

looked back and saw your mother's face go white,
saw her move as if to slap the hag, catch herself,
took, instead, your little hand, a bit too tightly,

and held it like that all the way home, saying only,
when you asked, "What is an *omen*, Mamma?"
Hush, child, do not take up what lost souls let drop.

The Language of the Grave

They died before the *Iliad* was first sung.
They died before that particular war
was fought, though war is war, that one
no more special in its day than all the little
bones of a child's ankles, mingled now, a handful
of the past. They ran once, and jumped for joy
when the river in spring flood brought
new bottomland to the fields. They were rich
with running. They were children. They had
no word for "desert." When they died,
their friends pleaded, *No, no, do not cover
them just yet*—and those children ran
and picked flowers and threw the flowers
into this strange, new hole that had opened
in their world. And even now, you can see
how slender their ankles were, and you can see
the fine layer of pollen, the finer layer of hope.

When We Ugly Women Die

...the death then of a beautiful woman is unquestionably the most poetical topic in the world.
    —*Edgar Allan Poe, "Philosophy of Composition"*

It is a relief. The waves, having never
missed a beat for us, can continue with
their heaving. The doves in the dovecote
can coo and coo, unmolested by images
of too-thin lips, flabby arms, and oh
those sagging breasts. Poor Clytemnestra,
pacing on her absent husband's parapets—
Stay out of the sun, one wants to tell her,
be more like Penelope to the north,
indoors all day weaving, chaste all night
with unweaving. But no, she would not
listen. A young lover gives her the illusion
of power. They plot ugly things, and at last
her leathery face twists beyond recognition
as she dies. When we ugly women die,
it isn't pretty. No mourning doves, just
the bat-winged, snake-haired, claw-footed
hags of justice, the escort to perdition,
dogs sniffing at the edges of the pool
of blood, slaves to mop up—or, rather,
a simple unstoried, unremembered grave
in a sea of unstoried, unremembered graves.

Joan of England's Portable Chapel

Five times a day, ten, she prays that her new husband
may be kind, perhaps may be at least a little handsome.
She loves her chapel, a birch-paneled closet built special
for this voyage. She will miss it when they disembark
in Spain. She knows that, long after she has donned
the gown with a thousand embroidered roses, long after
her own children are grown and married off and she
is dowager queen, she will remember her shipboard refuge.

That, ten days after landfall, she will be dead of plague,
her little chapel broken up to feed one of many fires
set to mask the stench—that this is soon to be,
she has no premonition. Her only fear is a storm
at sea, waves crashing over the deck of the ship
that transports her trousseau, the thousand roses
drenched, brittled by so much salt, a possible misfortune
that brings her once again to her knees, to pray.

The Fortune Teller

As she studies my palm, she does not foretell I'll one
day watch a tiny snail travel the length of my line
of life. Or that a dragonfly will accept my offer of a
landing pad, then change its mind, leaving only sunlight
in my upturned hand. She does not predict a future
fragrant with garden mint. What good the seer who
doesn't see the wasp that will tangle itself in my hair?
Or prophesize two goldfinches will appear from the
dark woods, and soar, at eye-level, past my head, one
on each side, leaving me startled at the wildness of my
own backyard, leaving me begging the silent woods, *Oh
tell me, tell me, what more is there to know?*

My Father, Photographing My Mother

They are not married yet. He tells her to sit
at the kitchen table. She is in a cotton housedress

and apron. *At least let me comb my hair.*
He does not. He wants her profile, her face turned

toward the window. Her shoulders say, *I have work
to do, do you want supper or not?* Her face

says, *what nonsense.* She holds still, chin raised
to the level of defiance. He does not care. It may be,

in fact, the expression he desired, just right
for the portrait he never painted.

Every Journey Ends in Prison

You come back eventually, and tell them
there's a whole other continent or something
in the way, or an ocean of sand, or mountains
that know no summer, and beasts of burden
the likes of which call into question
God's humor on that particular day
of creation. You come back and tell your friends
about the canyon washes, the height of the pines,
the roses, and they listen politely.
It is in the telling that you realize
I have returned, as if the journey never
happened, as if you imagined it all,
and that is what everyone else thinks, too.
Roses do not grow like that, with ease,
with abandon. There's a place for lunatics
such as you, a cell in which you can babble
stories to the walls, and the stones will answer
We know, we've been there, too.

She Talks about Teaching Herself How to Draw

No *camera lucida*, just a steady hand,
a good eye, the patience to see the position
of this relative to that, the first whorl
of the snail's shell to the next, to the next.

The acceptance of not good enough,
not precise. Throw the first attempt away
and begin anew. The second. Third.
The fourth almost right. Fifth.

A hundred times if need be. And needs
always are. Saying yes when he asked
me to marry him. All the new species
we'd find and describe. Saying no

when I realized he'd do the describing,
I'd be the one to draw. And cook. His name
for each discovery, mine there somewhere,
acknowledged, appreciated. No.

I've done my own drawing for fifty years.
For fifty years, I collect, I describe, I draw.
The operculum's a challenge,
making it look like something real.

Dashiell Hammett, Age 57, Reads *Jane Eyre* in the Ashland Federal Correctional Institution, Ashland, Kentucky, 1951

All told, it's not so bad. Five months,
easy labor mopping floors. His fellow inmates
say a man can do that time without hardly
changing socks. The prison farm provides
good food, bacon and eggs. And the library!
He's never read *Jane Eyre*, and though it's lights-out
at ten, he devours her, in one evening discovering
the dank of Lowood School—Jane's institution—
then the haunted Thornfield, before the lights
are cut. With the book beneath his pillow
he thinks of tomorrow, one long hall to scrub,
a chop for lunch, then more of Jane, already half
in love with one who knows how to survive
in this world, head down but eyes open,
just smile when someone spits where you
already mopped, just smile and mop again,
a third time even, smile and nod, if that's
all it takes to get back here, to get back home.

Reading Dostoevsky to the Girls

Not all of it. Just the chapter he happens to be on
when the girls, six and three, settle in next to him
on the sofa, so in love with his rare visits, so in love
with him. So of course, he wants to share this great thing,
Crime and Punishment, with them. *Then a strange idea
entered his head; that, perhaps, all his clothes
were covered with blood, that, perhaps, there were
a great many stains, but that he did not see them,
did not notice them because his perceptions were failing,
were going to pieces…* And the girls listen, afraid
to make a sound, for that might make him stop. Or worse,
leave. He is always leaving, it's always time to leave.
What is it, this too-great presence that must be left behind
to be even somewhat understood? Daddy's here.
Whatever he says, pretend you understand. What is it
makes the wrong things bigger than they are?
Makes wrong things, sometimes, right?

Mary Shelley Writing *Frankenstein*

Science? Let them think so. Let them think
I rail against the modern world, the too much
with us world, the world of learned astronomers
making us feel small. Byron used my sister
badly, but so do I, pulling her around Europe,
abandoning her when she is no longer useful.
My own children will die in my arms. My mother
died giving birth to me. Let them believe,
when I write of the miserable and the abandoned,
an abortion to be spurned at, and kicked,
and trampled on, let them believe I blame science.
I blame us, dear husbands, dearest lovers,
wretched fathers, I blame all of us together,
clawing at one another's beating hearts.

A Brief Life of John Keats

O for ten years, that I may overwhelm myself in poesy…
—Keats, "Sleep and Poetry"

Father owned a stable, came home smelling
of horses, manure mostly, but then,
those days, life was redolent of horses.
O damp, drafty, straw-specked, coal-powdered air,
O blood-spotted rags, hospital terrors—
how could I not turn to poesy? How could
I not become a watcher of the skies,
how not give myself to the influence
of some bright star, one bright morning star?
Physician, heal thyself—'tis not to be.
Say not, he could have out Chaucer'd Chaucer.
Balboa, Cortez—we each stand silent
on our solitary peak, as our sun
sinks into the Pacific, and day is done.

Luncheon with Henry James

Oblique allusions to his sister and her
sufferings. Oh how one longs to ask,
but a direct question, the merest intake
of breath before voicing "What exactly
ails her?" would send him skittering
sideways like a hat from a man dancing
a jig on a windy day, never to be seen
again. We take small bites. We sip.
The food is bland. He speaks of his brother,
both rationalist and mystic. Life, like art,
is less about what's there and more about
what isn't. Decipher your own days, if you
dare. She rarely leaves her room. I read
to her a little, though it exhausts us both.

What If Your Dentist Were Zane Grey?

The real Zane Grey, you know, had a degree
in dentistry, or what passed for dentistry
in 1896, and he practiced for a while, until
stories of the west began to fill his head

and he had to travel out to those wild places,
so next time your dentist's masked face
is inches from your own vulnerable self,
the little bib askew around your too-exposed

throat, you may wonder, is he imagining
some new Lassiter, driven by lost love
and the ability to kill, is he creating
in his head right now a world of heat

and stone and sage, dusty hooves
and brackish water, poisoned maybe,
and when he tells you to rinse and spit,
it sounds a lot like he's glad to see

the last of you, and needs a whiskey,
and as the metal tools clank in
the metal tray, his fingers tremble
just a little, just a very little bit.

William James and Sigmund Freud Walk to the Train Station, Worcester, Massachusetts, 1909

*Might I ask you to hold this for me, please, and
go on ahead?* he asks me in his noble, formal
German. I willingly become his valet. I proceed
slowly, pretend to examine a shoelace. I do not
look back to where I know James struggles
for a breath, waits for the *angina pectoris*
to subside. This portmanteau called the *body*
we lug around with us through life, all the while
chasing the weightless things of the mind—
the little we see of it in our dreams, knowing
we must spend our lives coming to terms
with its loss. *Dr. Freud*, he says, at my side
once more. *My apologies, kind sir, for the delay.*
How to tell him, it is no delay, holding
for a moment a hero's worldly goods, while he
steels himself for the final battle, shows us the way?

Eleven Reasons Not To Marry A Poet

*To you my dear Sister I leave all my things as they more
properly belong to you than any one.*
—first line of the alleged suicide note
of Harriet Shelley

1.
Poets are always underfoot, poetry being a solitary
occupation.

2.
Poets are never around when you need them, poetry
requiring numerous social occasions for the inspiration
thereof.

3.
The moping—the moping!

4.
You will want only frail, elderly landlords, faster than
whom you can run, better than whom you can see
at night, when you gather up all the children and
belongings to flee.

5.
The belongings will be few, but will include many books.

6.
The children will be many, but they will not want much and will mostly die young.

7.
Poets tend to die young, as well.

8.
Poets may live for decades beyond their best work, in which case they grow cranky.

9.
While always evoking the Spirit of Beauty, they never comb their hair.

10.
They are enamored of pretty words, but most especially of the saying of pretty words. You must be careful not to believe beyond the final iamb.

11.
When the poet abandons you for a better Muse, your own death will become a footnote in every anthology. Do not marry a poet unless you wish to see your name, in very, very, very fine print.

Adverbs

A very recent loss.
Lifelessly on the page.
Worriedly if they could see me.
Never.

A rather recent loss.
Gracefully down the road, I wish.
I always wish, though mostly silently.
Always.

A daily loss.
Away.
Quickly, always quickly.
Anywhere, so savagely.

Loss follows loyally at your heels.
Extravagantly. Ruthlessly.
Before this one, another.
After? So.

Our Maladies

The painful ones: bone shave, breakbone,
scrumpox. The occupational hazards:
potter's asthma, grocer's itch, dock fever.
All the ways to get typhus: jail fever,
ship fever, boarding house remorse.
Tuberculosis of the spine, lymph glands,
kidneys. Bloody sweat, bloody stools,
bloody mouth. Canker, catarrh, chorea.
Blackened, flushed, jaundiced. Pray
for our hopeless selves, Saint Jude,
Saint Adelard, Saint Bernadette.
Pray, Saint Anthony, for our poor
animal bodies, our weak flesh,
our pox, our flux, our chilblains,
a hundred names for syphilis,
a thousand ways to cough.

Emma Darwin's Prayer

"A sting in the eyeball wd. have been horrid."
—Emma Darwin, 1869

Your father, resting his injured leg, sits reading
in the drawing room—but see, though he is
immobile, nature seeks him out: a wasp
cannot resist the expansive Darwin brow.
I am afraid to move, to speak, to breathe,
but he does not flinch as the winged sprite
sips the very fluid from his eye! I pray—
not out loud, no, never out loud, of course—
all the while thinking this: that these words
need not ascend to heaven, need not rise
even to the level of the roofbeams, for God
is here with us (oh, your father would bristle
if he read this), yes, here with us, I say,
in this country house in Kent, on this spring day,
for this is heaven, and therefore God
must visit us, like the wasp, arriving and departing
unseen, but making its presence known
in such small but singular ways. Your father
has seen the world, seen sights few other men
have dreamt. I have seen an insect drink his tears.
Which one of us can say we have not seen God?
Which one of us can say we have not seen
how love manifests itself around us every day?

I allow one tear to escape down my cheek
as I watch your father become, in tiny measure,
the wasp. Is God so small he can offer only one destiny
to each of us? Perhaps we each have many, perhaps
we each take several paths, and somewhere
meet our several selves, and spend eternity
telling of the miracles we've seen.

Hyperbole

(thinking of John and Henry Donne)

The handsome young groomsman,
sent to shoot a sickly dog, shoots
himself instead, a terrible accident,
and the dog dies anyway the next afternoon.
The unmarried daughter of the household
takes to her bed with fevers, and she, too, dies;
it is whispered, heartbreak did her in.
Being paid to astonish and comfort with his words,
the poet takes the story of the maiden's demise,
though she was unknown to him, her loss
intangible, and regales it with all the import
her rich and grieving parents could desire.
Forgive the poet. He cannot write
of his own brother, rebel Catholic, dumped
into the common side of Newgate Prison
at the height of plague season, left to die
at no expense to the Crown. Let him write
of a lovely maiden taken "from this mortal sphere
to lively bliss," yes, let him speak of bliss,
let him assert that, with untimely death comes
not subtraction, but addition, a plus
to perfection, a gain to paradise.

Journey's End

A facile metaphor. Stale. Pedestrian.
Worst of all, common. Inadequate for
the thousands of miles—from the purchase
of gifts for every tribe to be encountered
along the way, to a winter with the Mandans,
the taste of horseflesh after a hungry week,
the sight of the Pacific, which was but
the half-way mark!—insufficient, this word
"journey," the brief word "end," but we
must employ them here for what little
we can imagine of the last few hours
of that life, Captain Meriwether Lewis
in the wilds of Tennessee, ranting,
pacing his room at Grinder's Inn,
sleepless, walking still, a life of walking,
thousands of miles, some by boat or horse,
but many on foot, a walk to the mouth
of the Columbia—as if this walk
haunted him, left him unable to stop,
the habit of movement having unhinged
his senses—and even then the end not easy,
this military man's final two shots somehow
off-target, one wounding his side, the other
shattering his skull, exposing brain, but not enough
to keep him from asking Mrs. Grinder for water,
or help—help at first to heal him, then help to find
someone to finish off the job—after thousands of miles,

the final one or two around the sorry grounds
of Grinder's Inn, somewhere in Tennessee,
a cool October night—the stars above,
the very ones that accompanied us on our way
across the known world, and out from it, and back—
common, uncommon, the word "journey," then
the little word that marks how, at last,
we give ourselves up to a little earthen bed.

Disembodied Gossip

—phrase used by Thomas Huxley to Alfred Russel Wallace to describe Spiritualism

And what do the spirits do, after successfully
spelling out your loved one's name backward,
to the astonishment of the person holding the pen,
who never 'til that moment knew whom it was
you sought? A rap upon the ceiling, followed
quickly by another from beneath the floor—
So many spirits visit us today, the medium
whispers. Suddenly the scribe drops the pen,
explaining, *It seemed to burn my hand,* showing
the red mark on his thumb. *John* he had written
on the page: *n h o j.* Several present are here
to speak to John—*Oh John, oh Jack, oh Johnny*
—one lady dabs a handkerchief to her eyes—
Keep your hands—the circle! Alas, too late.
They are dispersed, but the medium
can convey a little more: *They are all well.*
They are content to wait to see you again
some day, not soon. His limp is quite cured,
his cough as well. And yes, there are birds
of paradise in paradise, with plumage
more wondrous still. They perch on one's
outstretched hand. Even the naturalists
in the spirit realm rejoice that they
have crossed, have found the truth at last.

A Field Guide to the Spirits

The ones who were in pain have lost all memory of pain.

The ones who died while traveling are home.

The ones taken too young have attained the perfect age.

The ones who lingered a little too long—
              they tell us patience is the most blessed thing.

The ones who loved birds—
              you will feel their feather-touch.

The ones who lived in drafty houses, beneath roofs that
did not keep out rain, with smoky chimneys, mice in
the wainscotings, unreliable wells, never enough light,
crooked foundations, sagging joists—
              they dwell in comfort, and make
themselves known in the creaks of floorboard, rattle
of window, scent of smoke where there is no fire, and
especially the crack in the plaster shaped like the curve
of their lovely back.

There are ones who are like autumn: a nest with no
eggs, a fern too delicate for frost, an apple caught
between green and gold—
              they send the faintest signs, hesitant to
intrude on our still-growing world.

Change your hair. Change perfume, address, bedtime.
Change hatmaker, seamstress, physician. Start wearing
glasses, girdle, shirtwaist. The spirits understand the need
for change, and approve.

They ask little of us. Whisper their names, occasionally.
No one else need hear.

If one day you should find yourself in someone else's arms—
            the spirits understand the need for change.

The ones who were happy in life are happier still.

The ones who lacked all empathy in life—
            they are sorry.

They wish to tell you everything you ever longed to hear.

Author Biography

Jean LeBlanc, a New Englander transplanted to New Jersey, is the author of several collections and editor of two anthologies. She teaches English and facilitates writing workshops, always hoping to show the power of poetry to transport and transform. More of her work can be seen at www.jeanleblancpoetry.com.